Grow the Code

Student Workbook

William Collins' dream of knowledge for all began with the publication of his first book in 1819.
A self-educated mill worker, he not only enriched millions of lives, but also founded a flourishing publishing house.
Today, staying true to this spirit, Collins books are packed with inspiration, innovation and practical expertise.
They place you at the centre of a world of possibility and give you exactly what you need to explore it.

Published by Collins
An imprint of HarperCollins*Publishers*
The News Building, 1 London Bridge Street, London, SE1 9GF, UK

HarperCollins*Publishers*
Macken House, 39/40 Mayor Street Upper, Dublin 1, D01 C9W8, Ireland

Browse the complete Collins catalogue at
collins.co.uk

© Wandle Learning Trust 2026
littlewandlecode.org.uk

10 9 8 7 6 5 4 3 2 1

A catalogue record for this publication is available from the British Library.

ISBN 978-0-00-879103-2

All rights reserved. No part of this publication may be reproduced, stored in a retrieval system, or transmitted in any form by any means, electronic, mechanical, photocopying, recording or otherwise, without the prior written permission of the Publisher or a licence permitting restricted copying in the United Kingdom issued by the Copyright Licensing Agency Ltd, 5th Floor, Shackleton House, 4 Battle Bridge Lane, London SE1 2HX.

Without limiting the exclusive rights of any author, contributor or the publisher of this publication, any unauthorised use of this publication to train generative artificial intelligence (AI) technologies is expressly prohibited. HarperCollins also exercise their rights under Article 4(3) of the Digital Single Market Directive 2019/790 and expressly reserve this publication from the text and data mining exception.

Little Wandle Code has been developed by
Wandle Learning Trust in collaboration with Collins.

At Wandle Learning Trust:
Author: Sarah Paxton
Project manager: Rachel Russ
Editors: Helen Lawson, Caroline Hale, Tracy Kewley
Proofreaders: Jane Jackson, Jennie Clifford
Cover designer: Communitas
Internal designers and typesetters: Communitas, Tech-Set

At Collins:
Publisher: Katie Sergeant
Product manager: Natasha Paul
Production controller: Sophie Waeland

Printed in the UK

Acknowledgements

The publishers gratefully acknowledge the permission granted to reproduce the copyright material in this book. Every effort has been made to trace copyright holders and to obtain their permission for the use of copyright material. The publishers will gladly receive any information enabling them to rectify any error or omission at the first opportunity.

Mnemonic illustrations by Noah Warnes
Other illustrations by Marek Jagucki, apart from
p. 7: New Vectors/Shutterstock

Contents

Unit 1 (Sessions 1.1 to 1.4)	5
Unit 2 (Sessions 2.1 to 2.4)	9
Unit 3 (Sessions 3.1 to 3.4)	15
Unit 4 (Sessions 4.1 to 4.4)	21
Unit 5 (Sessions 5.1 to 5.4)	27
Unit 6 (Sessions 6.1 to 6.4)	33
Unit 7 (Sessions 7.1 to 7.4)	39
Unit 8 (Sessions 8.1 to 8.4)	45
Unit 9 (Sessions 9.1 to 9.4)	51
Unit 10 (Sessions 10.1 to 10.4)	57
Grow the Code Chart	70
Glossary	72

Session 1.1

Table 1

	👉	✍️
sun	3	sun
zip		
splat		
laptop		

Table 2

	👉	✍️
wish		
chicken		
umbrella		
light		

Session 1.3

Table 1

	👆
cabin	2
shelf	
address	
magnetic	
significant	

Table 2

	👆	Prefix	Word	Suffix
jumping	2		jump	ing
sadness				
misspell				
unfit				
untested				

Session 1.4
You as a Reader

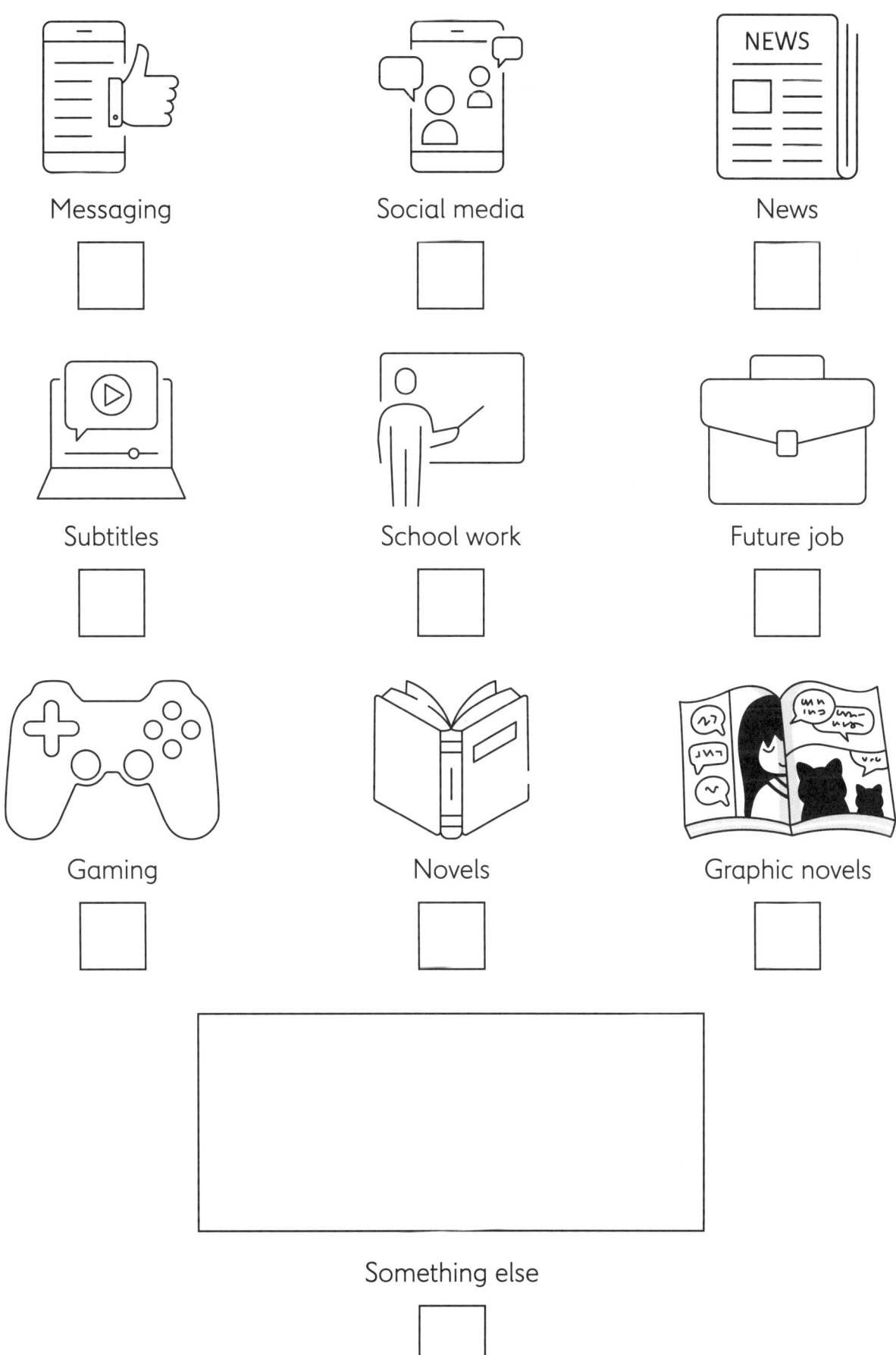

Code Agreement

I agree to:

- Follow instructions

- Listen to my teacher

- Be kind to my peers

- Not give up, even when it is hard

- Remember that mistakes help me learn

- Ask for help if I need it

- Take my reading learning seriously.

Signed _____

Session 2.1 ai

Map it

ff	h	th	u
r	nk	ch	w
ng	l	z	sh

Learn Curriculum Words

1. _____

2. _____

3. _____

4. _____

Spell it: Add it

Word	Suffix	New Word	
complain		complained	2
claim	ed		
contain			
explain			

Summary

ai	Review			
claim	think	spring	wing	
contain	drank	rang	bring	
afraid	shrank	drink	sprang	
explained	rink	thank	bang	
complained	thing	shrink		
claimed	ring	sink		
explain				
contained				
complain				

Session 2.2 ee

Map it

zz	b	ck	ai
ng	sh	f	mm
ll	th	qu	nk

Learn Curriculum Words

1. _____

2. _____

3. _____

4. _____

Spell it: Add it

Word	Suffix	New Word	👆
speed	ed	speeded	2
tweet			
wait			
paint			

Summary

ee	Review		
speed	pain	chain	wait
freedom	rain	brain	waited
screen	train	trail	tail
tweet	jail	them	then
speeded	than	thin	paint
tweeted	think	thick	painted
chimpanzee	thump	thud	

Session 2.4

Code it

wind	chunk	week
mend	sheep	pain
kick	snail	shop
long	fizz	greed
raindrop	seed	trail
sand	splash	cracking
toffee	strain	stump
maintain	treetop	speech
thick	packet	sprint
painting	spring	cheek

Make it

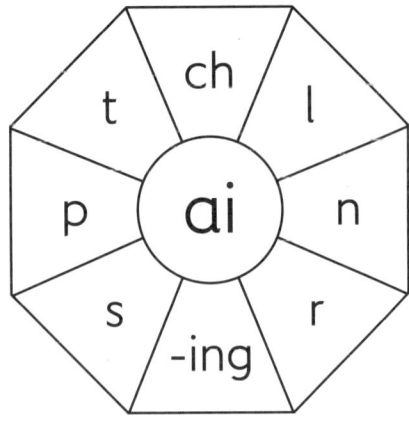 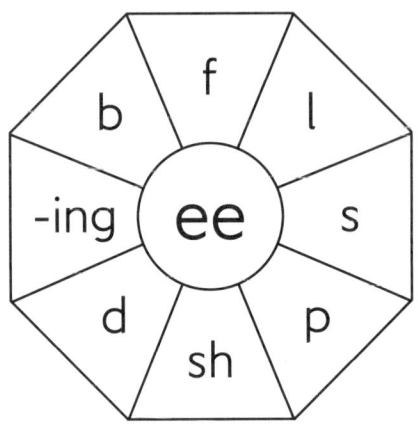

Hints:
1. When it _ _ _ _ _, I need an umbrella.
2. The dog wagged its _ _ _ _.
3. If you get ink on your top, it will _ _ _ _ _.

Hints:
1. buzzing insects = _ _ _ _
2. the skin of an apple = _ _ _ _
3. I cut myself and it is _ _ _ _ _ _ _ _.

Session 3.1 igh

Map it

e	qu	ch	ee
x	y	ai	sh
ng	v	j	w

Learn Curriculum Words

1. _____

2. _____

3. _____

4. _____

Spell it: Add it

Word	Suffix	New Word	👆
highlight	ing	highlighting	3
fight			
screech			
train			

Summary

igh	Review		
highlight	tree	three	screech
fight	free	freed	screeching
bright	greed	weed	seed
midnight	sail	speed	train
highlighting	snail	nail	training
fighting	strain	stain	pain
lightning	plain	sprain	

Session 3.2 oa

Map it

ch	y	w	th
sh	u	ll	igh
ee	ai	b	ss

Learn Curriculum Words

1. _____

2. _____

3. _____

4. _____

Spell it: Add it

Word	Suffix	New Word	
soak	ed	soaked	1
croak			
coach			
peek			

Summary

oa	Review		
boast soak	sight	night	might
coastal soaked	light	fight	fright
croak croaked	bright	right	stain
float coached	saint	faint	paint
coach cockroach	painting	sheet	greet
	street	sweet	tweet
	peek	peeked	

Session 3.4

Code it

throat	flight	trust
buzz	shrank	bench
raincoat	asleep	float
swing	oak	nights
croak	upright	brain
sight	sprain	sniff
rail	frighten	lightning
thing	coaching	roam
drench	bright	waiting
blinking	speedboat	liquid

Make it

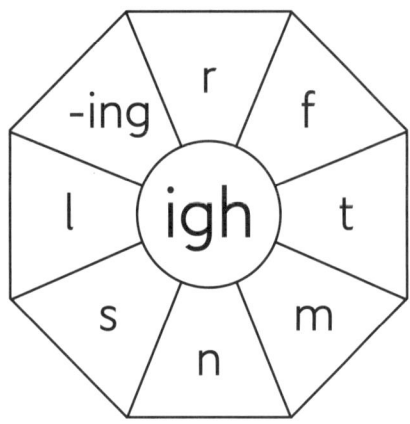

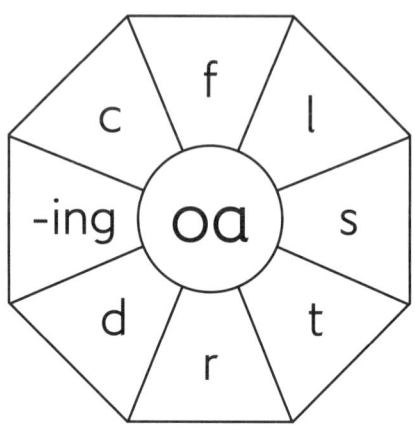

Hints:
1. when you sleep = _ _ _ _ _
2. something you see = _ _ _ _ _
3. lamp - _ _ _ _ _

Hints:
1. jacket = _ _ _ _
2. like a frog = _ _ _ _
3. street = _ _ _ _

Session 4.1 er

Map it

ee	oa	o	th
ai	nk	h	ch
ng	z	g	igh

Learn Curriculum Words

1. _____

2. _____

3. _____

4. _____

Spell it: Add it

Word	Suffix	New Word	👆
bright	er	brighter	2
high			
soft			
sweet			

Summary

er		Review		
pattern brighter		oak	cloak	coat
copper higher		boat	boast	coast
expert softer		roast	roasting	fright
chapter sweeter		flight	slight	light
		sunlight	see	seem
		seed	speed	speedboat
		bright	high	soft
		sweet		

Session 4.2 ar

Map it

x	ck	b	igh
w	ff	ee	ss
ai	er	sh	oa

Learn Curriculum Words

1. _____

2. _____

3. _____

4. _____

Spell it: Add it

Word	Suffix	New Word	👆
sharp		sharpest	2
hard	est		
dark			
harsh			

Summary

ar	Review		
Antarctica dark	her	herb	kerb
artist harsh	term	stern	finger
landmark sharpest	river	number	oak
starfish hardest	oat	coat	boat
sharp darkest	sailboat	sight	sigh
hard harshest	high	thigh	tight

Session 4.4

Code it

verb	fright	scarf
alarm	painting	slight
heel	coax	soak
might	chart	landmark
artist	expert	oat
stern	boast	term
cloak	sunlight	seem
street	kerb	coast
farmyard	roasting	start
river	under	charm

Make it

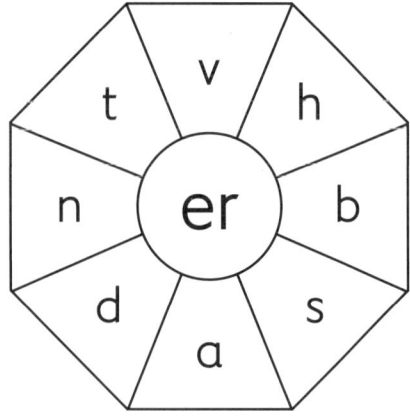
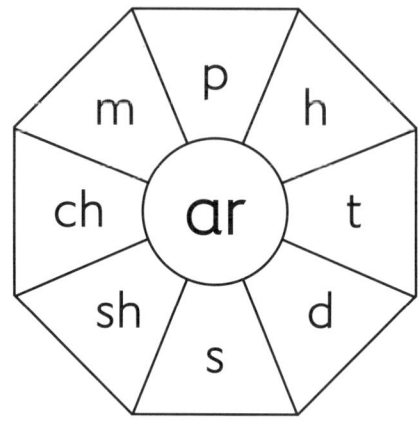

Hints:
1. plants you add to a dish = _ _ _ _ _
2. a lot of cows = _ _ _ _
3. strict = _ _ _ _ _

Hints:
1. not blunt = _ _ _ _ _
2. the red planet = _ _ _ _
3. Your hand is at the end of your _ _ _.

Session 5.1 ur

Map it

sh	c	t	ll
ar	er	ee	ck
igh	oa	k	ai

Learn Curriculum Words

1. _____

2. _____

3. _____

4. _____

Spell it: Add it

Word	Suffix	New Word	👆
church	es	churches	2
coach			
fox			
dish			

Summary

ur	Review		
blurb	mark	hark	shark
disturb	spark	park	apart
nocturnal	start	chart	printer
church	partner	painter	toaster
churches	chapter	soak	croak
	cloak	oak	oat
	coach	coaches	fox
	foxes	dish	dishes

Session 5.2 or

Map it

ai	nk	oa	th
ar	ee	ur	igh
v	ch	qu	zz

Learn Curriculum Words

1. _____

2. _____

3. _____

4. _____

Spell it: Add it

Word	Prefix	New Word	👆
portrait	self-	self-portrait	3
esteem			
confident			
respect			

Summary

or	Review		
important portrait absorb export self-portrait	turn burst blurt arch marker spinner esteem confident	churn burp blurb march dinner spanner self-esteem self-confident	burn blur arm mark winner planner respect self-respect

Session 5.4

Code it

u̲n f̲u̲r̲l̲	toaster	nocturnal
chapter	cheep	flex
flick	orbit	disturb
herd	splat	burn
spotlight	acorn	afford
pondweed	thorn	partner
march	export	scrunch
order	short	winter
blurb	hurt	thrill
morning	churn	raiding

Make it

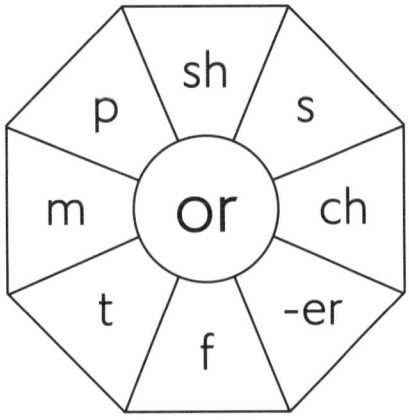

Hints:
1. cricket, golf or badminton
   = _ _ _ _ _
2. handheld light = _ _ _ _ _
3. thunder and lightning = _ _ _ _ _

Hints:
1. If it is painful, it _ _ _ _ _.
2. pop = _ _ _ _ _
3. you have this in a bun, with relish
   = _ _ _ _ _ _

Session 6.1 oo

Map it

j	g	igh	er
ee	ar	oa	or
ai	ll	f	h

Learn Curriculum Words

1. _____

2. _____

3. _____

4. _____

Spell it: Add it

Word	Suffix	New Word	👆
dark	ness	darkness	2
sad			
ill			
bright			

Summary

oo	Review			
smooth mushroom cartoon moonlight	born scorn turn burn harm sad bright	corn sport disturb scar alarm sadness brightness	torn port suburb scarf dark ill	storm export church cart darkness illness

Session 6.2 oo

Map it

oo	b	ur	w
igh	ss	ee	oa
y	ar	ai	or

Learn Curriculum Words

1. _____

2. _____

3. _____

4. _____

Spell it: Add it

Word	Suffix	New Word	
look	ed	looked	1
book			
hack			
check			

Summary

oo	Review			
wooden footprint cooker bookmark look book looked booked	moo pool stork short breed check	mood tool fork beep freed checked	food stool fort bleep hack	fool toolbox sort bleed hacked

Session 6.4

Code it

slept	shook	approach
starfish	footprint	cartoon
smooth	harp	teeth
drooping	cling	tool
furnish	good	crook
afraid	doom	sworn
gloom	export	coastal
cooker	coffee	stood
mermaid	tooth	highland
murmur	hood	scoop

Make it

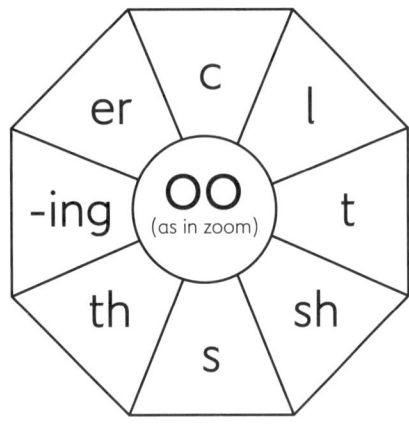 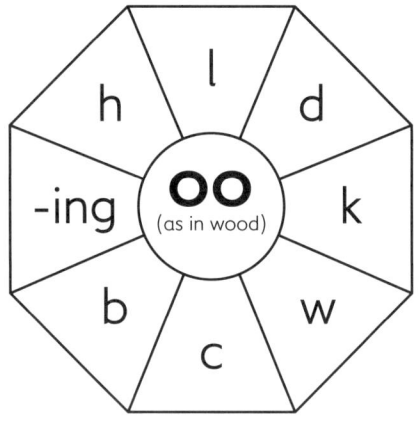

Hints:
1. not hot = _ _ _ _
2. as well = _ _ _
3. spanner, hammer and drill
   = _ _ _ _ _

Hints:
1. sheep's fur = _ _ _ _
2. seeing = _ _ _ _ _ _ _
3. I am _ _ _ _ _ _ _ dinner.

Session 7.1 ow

Map it

oo	or	ar	oa
er	ee	qu	ch
sh	th	igh	ai

Learn Curriculum Words

1. _____

2. _____

3. _____

4. _____

Spell it: Add it

Word	Suffix	New Word	👆
download		downloading	3
frown	ing		
prowl			
flower			

Summary

ow		Review		
crowd	prowl	good	hood	hook
power	download	look	looking	booking
downloading	frown	bookshelf	book	port
frowning	tower	porch	torch	thorn
prowling	flower	north	toad	toast
flowering		roast	boast	road

Session 7.2 oi

Map it

oa	ee	ng	oo
ow	ar	ur	or
ai	igh	ff	ll

Learn Curriculum Words

1. _____

2. _____

3. _____

4. _____

Spell it: Add it

Word	Suffix	New Word	👏
point	less	pointless	2
power			
harm			
pain			

Summary

oi	Review			
boiling	owl	cow	bow	brown
avoid	frown	drown	down	download
point	swoop	scoop	spoon	smooth
asteroid	shoot	order	border	barber
pointless	better	letter	power	powerless
	pain	painless	harm	harmless

Session 7.4

Code it

c̲l̲o̲w̲n̲	fool	brush
brink	looking	howl
join	spoil	avoid
stark	zookeeper	curl
powder	download	boiling
freed	higher	bookshelf
appoint	herb	scowl
corner	tinfoil	aimless
power	booth	bitcoin
rabbit	crown	growling

Make it

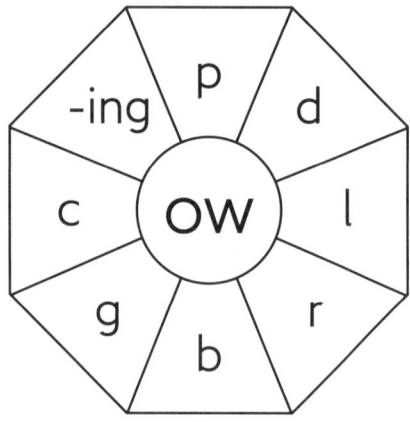
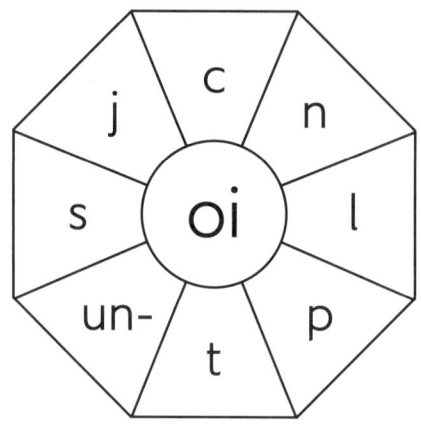

___

___

___

___

___

___

___

___

___

___

___

___

___

___

Hints:
1. farm animal = _ _ _
2. disagreement = _ _ _
3. An _ _ _ hoots at night.

Hints:
1. you can spend this; it is metal = _ _ _ _
2. a bit like mud = _ _ _ _
3. liquid needed for cooking = _ _ _

Session 8.1 air

Map it

sh	oo	igh	oa
er	ee	ar	or
ow	oi	th	ai

Learn Curriculum Words

1. _____

2. _____

3. _____

4. _____

Spell it: Add it

Word	Prefix	New Word	👆
fair		unfair	2
lock	un		
seen			
afraid			

Summary

air	Review			
unfair	join	coin	coil	foil
fair	boil	soil	spoil	spoilt
airport	crowd	crown	frown	town
upstairs	down	soot	foot	took
repair	cook	cooker	lock	unlock
	seen	unseen	afraid	unafraid

Session 8.2 ear

Map it

ar	ee	ch	oi
oa	igh	nk	ai
ow	ur	oo	air

Learn Curriculum Words

1. _____

2. _____

3. _____

4. _____

Spell it: Add it

Word	Prefix	New Word	👆
appear		disappear	3
connect	dis		
agree			
infect			

Summary

ear	Review			
appear	air	hair	pair	lair
unclear	stair	chair	armchair	highchair
disappear	boil	boiling	boing	oink
spear	oil	howl	prowl	scowl
eardrum	clown	drown	connect	disconnect
	agree	disagree	infect	disinfect

Session 8.4

Code it

chair	rear	wood
spoilt	brand	scorn
gear	clear	frown
repairs	bloom	dear
earmuff	windmill	disappear
airlift	trailing	lair
stairs	charcoal	flair
flower	despair	beard
glinting	coin	highchair
coil	beekeeper	frown

Make it

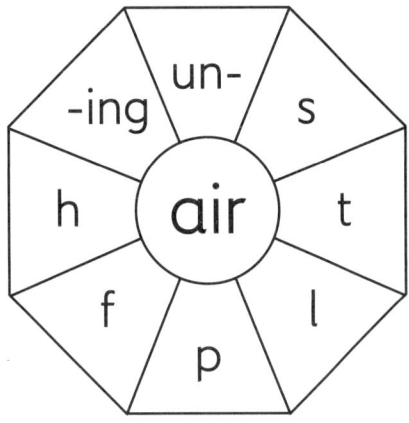

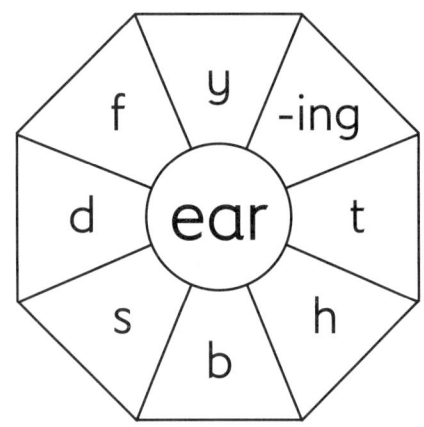

Hints:
1. steps = _ _ _ _ _ _
2. I picked a _ _ _ _ of boots at the shop.
3. I had my _ _ _ _ cut by the barber.

Hints:
1. hair on a man's chin = _ _ _ _ _
2. how to start a letter = _ _ _ _
3. fright = _ _ _ _

Session 9.1 /ch/ ch, tch, ture

Map it

ear	c	l	k
ll	air	er	oa
ck	oi	ow	igh

Learn New Code

ch	tch	ture
chip	hutch	picture
'ch' can appear anywhere in a word. When a word starts with /ch/, it is always spelled 'ch'.	'tch' never appears at the beginning of a word. It is usually found at the end of a word. It is rarely found the middle (only in words like 'kitchen' or 'ketchup').	'ture' always the end

Spell it: Add it

Word	Suffix	New Word	👆
glitch		glitches	2
match	es		
dress			
speech			

Summary

/ch/ ch, tch, ture	Review		
chip hutch	ear	hear	near
picture glitch	fear	dear	year
mixture kitchen	tear	teardrop	air
sculpture glitches	airport	airbag	airlift
match matches	airmail	join	coil
speech speeches	boiling	tinfoil	avoid
	dress	dresses	

Session 9.2 /n/ n, kn

Map it

ture	ss	ch	th
tch	g	air	ow
s	oi	nk	t

Learn New Code

n	kn
nest	knit
'n' is by far the most common way to spell /n/.	'kn' is an unusual spelling for /n/. It only appears at the beginning of a word.

Spell it: Add it

Word	Suffix	New Word	👆
knight	ed	knighted	2
sprint			
point			
knit			

Summary

/n/ n, kn		Review		
kneel	nest	stitch	switch	twitch
knight	knit	pitch	patch	matchbox
knock	knighted	catch	match	year
number	knitted	fear	hear	spear
		earring	chair	pair
		unfair	repairs	downstairs
		sprint	sprinted	point
		pointed		

Session 9.4

Code it

hair	snarl	batch
capture	chess	kneecap
knelt	lunch	etch
bitten	knotted	supper
grab	mixture	sketch
airship	hopscotch	screen
dear	spinach	picture
knack	knitting	lighter
bonnet	near	matchbook
hitch	stunt	sculpture

Make it

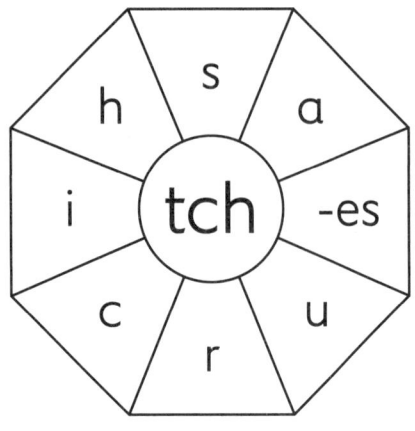 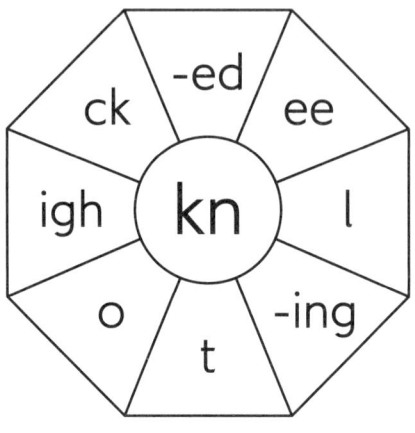

Hints:
1. you need this if you hurt your leg = _ _ _ _ _ _
2. The sharp thorns might _ _ _ _ _ _ _ you.
3. My pet rabbit lives in a _ _ _ _ _.

Hints:
1. bang with your fist = _ _ _ _ _
2. The _ _ _ _ _ _ held a spear.
3. Put a _ _ _ _ in the string.

Session 10.1 /r/ r, wr

Map it

th	ture	z	ch
ear	n	zz	x
u	kn	tch	v

Learn New Code

r	wr
rush	wreck
'r' is by far the most common way to spell /r/.	'wr' is an unusual spelling for /r/. It only appears at the beginning of a word.

Spell it: Add it

Word	Prefix	New Word	
wrap		unwrap	2
clear	un		
well			
important			

Summary

/r/ r, wr	Review			
wrong	knee	kneel	knelt	
random	knight	knock	knot	
wrist	knit	knitted	catch	
wrap	hatch	hitch	itch	
unwrap	itching	north	port	
rush	porch	torch	thorn	
wreck	clear	unclear	unwell	
	important	unimportant	well	

Session 10.2 /w/ wh and /f/ ph

Map it

n	ai	tch	ture
air	b	oi	g
ch	ear	th	kn

Learn New Code

wh	ph
whisk	graph
'wh' is a less common spelling for /w/. It only appears at the beginning of a word.	'ph' is a less common spelling for /f/. It can appear at the beginning, in the middle or at the end of a word.

Spell it: Add it

Word	Suffix	New Word	👆
stress		stressful	2
power	ful		
pain			
fear			

Summary

/w/ wh and /f/ ph	Review		
when graph	wrist	wrap	wriggle
wheel paragraph	wrong	wrinkle	wreck
whisk alphabet	knock	knot	knight
	kneecap	witch	knee
	stitch	stretch	switch
	stress	stressful	matching
	powerful	pain	power
	fearful	fear	painful

Session 10.4

Code it

arch	graph	summer
catching	junk	burnt
knitted	wrapper	morph
shipwreck	freewheel	cork
wren	whizz	trinket
alphabet	trench	exit
shrink	whisker	button
shower	humph	quill
thatch	whoosh	wrench
written	shorts	paragraph

Make it

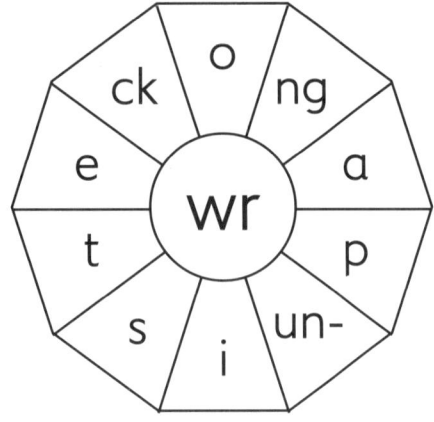 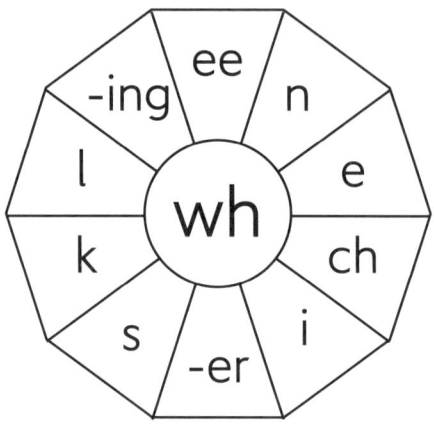

_____

_____

_____

_____

_____

_____

_____

Hints:
1. You _ _ _ _ _ _ a present.
2. part of your arm = _ _ _ _ _
3. The ship sank. It was a _ _ _ _ _.

Hints:
1. part of a car = _ _ _ _ _
2. Mix up eggs with a _ _ _ _ _.
3. long hairs on a cat's cheeks
   = _ _ _ _ _ _ _ _

Grow the Code Chart

Consonants

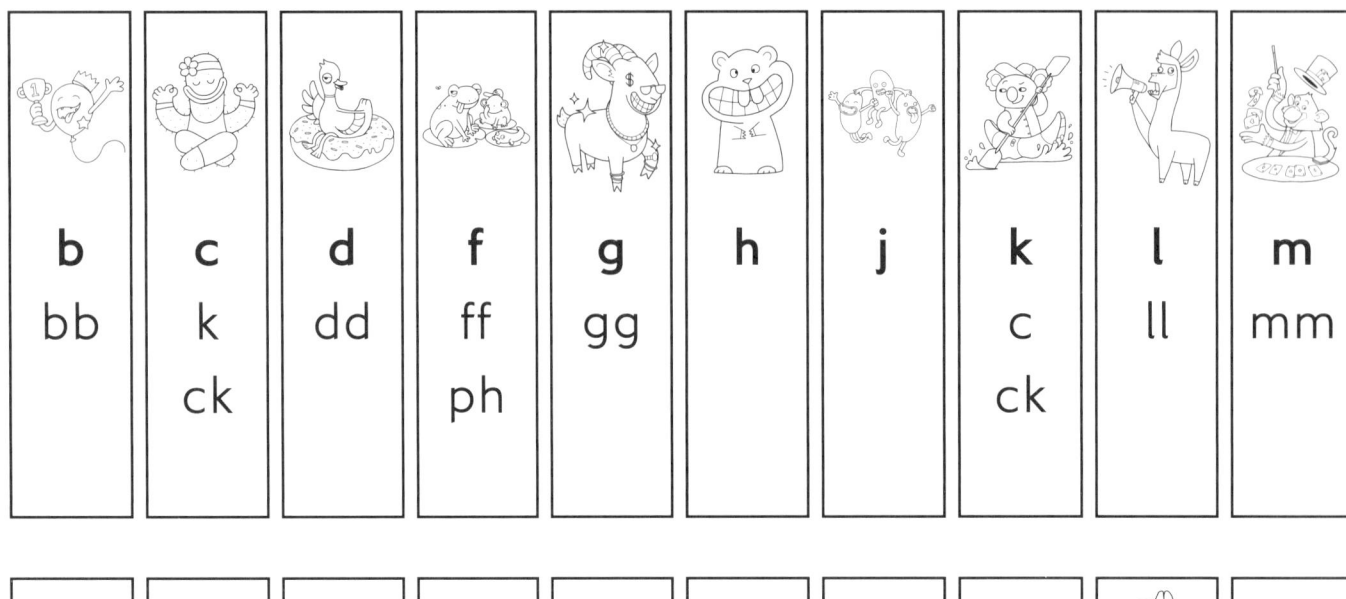

b	c	d	f	g	h	j	k	l	m
bb	k	dd	ff	gg			c	ll	mm
	ck		ph				ck		

n	p	r	s	t	v	w	x	y	z
nn	pp	rr	ss	tt		wh			zz
kn		wr							

Consonant Digraphs

ch	ng	nk	qu	sh	th
tch					
ture*					

*This has a slight schwa at the end, 'chuh'.

Glossary

blend: We blend phonemes together to make a word. For example, c-a-t is blended together to make the word 'cat'.

code it out loud: When we code a word out loud, we say each of the phonemes in the word. For example, the word 'cat' coded out is c-a-t.

digraph: Two letters that together make one phoneme (sound). For example, the digraph 'sh' makes the sound /sh/ in the word 'shot'.

grapheme: A letter, or group of letters, that represents a phoneme (sound). For example, the word 'cat' has three graphemes: 'c', 'a' and 't'.

phoneme: A sound within a word. For example, there are three phonemes in the word 'cat': /c/, /a/, /t/.

prefix: A group of letters we add to the start of a word to change its meaning. For example, 'rewrite' is 'write' with 're-' added at the beginning, so 're-' is the prefix.

schwa: An unstressed vowel sound that is in a lot of words. It sounds a bit like 'uh'. For example, in the word 'doctor', the second vowel sound is a schwa. In 'elephant', the final vowel sound is a schwa.

suffix: A group of letters we add to the end of a word to change its meaning. For example, 'playing' is 'play' + '-ing', so '-ing' is the suffix.

syllable: A beat of sound within a word. For example, the word 'sunset' has two syllables: 'sun' and 'set'.

tricky word: A common word that cannot be decoded easily because it contains one or more unusual graphemes. For example, in the word 'of', the grapheme 'f' makes the sound /v/.

trigraph: Three letters that together make one phoneme (sound). For example, the trigraph 'igh' makes the sound /igh/ in the word 'night'.

tweak it: When we tweak it, we slightly adjust how we say a word to make it sound right. For example, for 'doctor', we say 'doct-UH' not 'doct-OR'.

Vowels

| a | e | i | o | u |

Vowel Digraphs and Trigraphs

| ai | air | ar | ear | ee | er | igh |

| oa | oi | oo | oo | or | ow | ur |

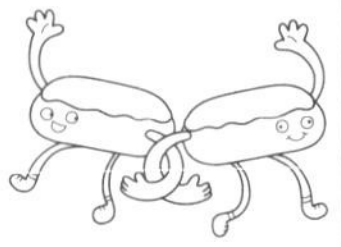